The Pool Activity Level (PAL) Instrument for Occupational Profiling

of related interest

The Perspectives of People with Dementia
Research Methods and Motivations
Edited by Heather Wilkinson
ISBN 1 84310 001 0

Training and Development for Dementia Care Workers
Anthea Innes
ISBN 1 85302 761 8

Healing Arts Therapies and Person-Centred Dementia Care
Edited by Anthea Innes and Karen Hatfield
ISBN 1 84310 038 X

Primary Care and Dementia
Steve Illife and Vari Drennan
Foreword by Murna Downs
ISBN 1 85302 997 1
Bradford Dementia Group Good Practice Guides

Choosing Assistive Devices
A Guide for Users and Professionals
Helen Pain, D. Lindsay McLellan and Sally Gore
ISBN 185302 985 8

The Care Homes Legal Handbook
Jeremy Cooper
ISBN 1 84310 064 9

Hearing the Voice of People with Dementia
Opportunities and Obstacles
Malcolm Goldsmith
ISBN 1 85302 406 6

The Pool Activity Level (PAL) Instrument for Occupational Profiling

A Practical Resource for Carers of People with Cognitive Impairment, Second Edition

Jackie Pool

Jessica Kingsley Publishers
London and Philadelphia

The right of Jackie Pool to be identified as author of this work has been asserted by her in accordance with the Copyright, Designs and Patents Act 1988

First edition published in 1999
by Jessica Kingsley Publishers
This edition published in the United Kingdom
in 2002 by Jessica Kingsley Publishers Ltd
116 Pentonville Road
London N1 9JB, England
and
325 Chestnut Street
Philadelphia
PA 19106, USA

www.jkp.com

Copyright © Jackie Pool 2002

Library of Congress Cataloging in Publication Data

A CIP catalog record for this book is available from the Library of Congress

British Library Cataloguing in Publication Data

A CIP catalogue record for this book is available from the British Library

ISBN 1 84310 080 0

Printed and Bound in Great Britain by
Athenaeum Press, Gateshead, Tyne and Wear

Contents

Contents

Preface

The Pool Activity Level (PAL) Instrument was first published in 1999 as a part of the Good Practice Guide series from the Bradford Dementia Group. It is intended as a practical resource for carers of people with cognitive impairments which may cause dementia and other disabilities. This guidebook is designed to enable carers at home and in formal care settings to use the Pool Activity Level (PAL) Instrument to engage people with cognitive impairment in meaningful occupation.

The PAL Instrument was originally developed for use with people with dementia. It is now being used widely in health and social services care establishments and in community settings in the UK and around the world. Some users of the PAL are finding it effective for clients other than those with dementia and are using it to form occupational profiles for people who have had strokes and those with learning disabilities.

Feedback from departments and individuals has been very positive about the use of the PAL. For example, Cambridgeshire County Council Social Services introduced the use of the PAL Instrument in 1999 to develop their services to people with dementia in their residential settings. The strategy was so successful that Cambridge Social Services have won a best practice award and have gone on to implement the use of the PAL Instrument in home care settings and in services for people with learning disabilities.

The Brent, Kensington, Chelsea and Westminster Mental Health NHS Trust have introduced the PAL Instrument as their basis for using an activity-based model of care in their continuing care wards. A recent one-year study of the activity provision in four of their establishments, by the National Association of Providers of Activities, gave high praise to the PAL Instrument.

Current position

Feedback from users of the PAL Instrument has been useful in highlighting areas that need to be refined. These were that the Checklist needed to have the same number of, and similar, statements for each level of ability; that the clients often have different levels of ability in different tasks (depending on familiarity with the task); that the Action Plans needed to be more individualized and that there needs to be an outcome sheet.

Refinements have been made taking into account the feedback information and a new version of the Checklist and Action Plans has been piloted with Cambridgeshire Social Services. Their response to the new version was very positive. A statement from their training manager reads: 'I have trained 50 staff with the new PAL and find it excellent. A great improvement, it's easier, great to put into care notes and altogether better. I will train all my key dementia practice trainers (60) to take it back into the workplace.'

This second edition of the PAL is the result of the feedback from many care workers, and I would particularly like to thank the following individuals and services for their constructive criticism and kind help in the development of this instrument: the members of the Haslemere branch of the Alzheimer's Society; Sue Owen and the social services training section of Cambridgeshire County Council; Sharon Parsons and the occupational therapy department at the Maitland Assessment Unit of the East London and The City Mental Health NHS Trust.

1 Introduction

Using this Guide

The PAL Instrument is based on the underpinning principle that people with cognitive impairment also have abilities and that when an enabling environment is presented to the person, these potential abilities can be realised. Occupation is the key to unlocking this potential. In order to present an occupation to the person with cognitive impairment so that he or she can engage with it, his or her impairments and abilities must first be understood. In addition, an individual is motivated to engage in occupations that have personal significance. Therefore an understanding of what drives the person, using information about his or her unique biography and about personality, is also vital. The PAL Instrument provides the user with the means to collect this important information and to use it to compile an individual profile that aids in the presentation of occupations to the person.

The PAL Instrument comprises:

- Life History Profile
- Checklist describing the way that an individual engages in occupations
- Activity Profile with general information for engaging the person in a range of meaningful occupations
- Individual Action Plan that includes directions for facilitating the engagement of the person in activities of daily living
- Outcome Sheet.

A blank copy of the PAL Instrument is in this guidebook and may be photocopied for use by those working with people with cognitive impairment.

Theoretical Background

The Pool Activity Level (PAL) Instrument draws from several models of understanding human behaviour: the Lifespan Approach to human development; the Dialectical Model of a person-centred approach to the interplay of social, neurological and psychological factors; and the Cognitive Disability Model.

The Lifespan Approach to Human Development

Theorists of human development propose that individuals' physical, intellectual, social and emotional skills change over time, according to the experiences they encounter. When this process is viewed in this way it is termed the Lifespan Approach. The first major theorist to acknowledge the lifelong nature of human development was Erik Erikson (Atkinson, Atkinson and Hilgard 1983) who described the 'Eight Ages of Man', each of which presents the individual with a new developmental task to be worked on. Erikson proposed that human development does not end when physical maturity is reached, but that it is a continuous process from birth through to old age. His eight stages were based on the belief that the psychological development of an individual depends on the social relations he or she experiences at various points in life. When working with people with cognitive impairment it is helpful not only to recognize the importance of this cradle-to-grave development theory but also to understand some of the developmental processes which take place in infancy and childhood. A more detailed description of developmental theory can be found elsewhere, but a brief description of neurological development is included here in order to clarify the theory underpinning the PAL Instrument.

When a child is born, the higher part of the brain is like a blank page waiting to be written on as experiences are encountered. The higher part of the brain is concerned with cognition, which includes functions such as thought, judgement, comprehension and reasoning. It also controls complex functions such as processing information from the environment sent from the sensory organs – the eyes, ears, nose, mouth and skin – via the nervous system to the brain. Infants learn from these experiences which are 'written on' to the higher brain as memories in the form of patterns of nerve connections. This enables infants to judge new experiences against previous ones and to make decisions about how to respond. They also begin to be able to adapt to new situations as they arise by matching the experience to similar ones. It is a function of the higher brain to interpret information and to decide on the necessary action.

At first, the new-born baby is relying on the more primitive underlying part of the brain, which is concerned with basic emotions and needs. This primitive brain is responsible for early behaviour such as fear of strangers and the forming of a bond or specific attachment with another person. It also causes individuals, throughout their life, to experience and communicate social-emotional nuances (via emotional speech, laughing, crying, expressing sympathy, compassion) and to desire to form and maintain an emotional attachment. The primitive brain therefore enables us to be what is essentially a person: to establish the identity and existence that is conferred on us through contact with others.

The Dialectical Model of a Person-centred Approach

This model was proposed by Tom Kitwood when exploring factors other than neurological impairment that combine to cause the disability of dementia. One way of viewing these factors is as an equation where $D = P + B + H + NI + SP$ (Kitwood 1993). This is a simple way of showing that any individual's dementia (D) is the result of a complex interaction between five main components: personality (P), biography (B), health (H), neurological impairment (NI) and social psychology (SP). To view dementia only as a result of the neurological impairment caused by the medical picture of Alzheimer's disease, for example, would be to view an incomplete picture. An individual's personality and life history will colour and shape the picture, although for the most part these will have been fully developed and are unchangeable.

Physical and mental ill health often cause people to behave differently as they try to cope with feelings of pain or discomfort. Some people with neurological impairments are unable to communicate their need to others verbally. Their behaviour, which is another form of communication, can be misinterpreted as part of their condition and the inappropriate response from others contributes further to the disability of the individual.

The final component of social psychology in the equation is viewed as the one that can have the most significant impact, either for better or worse. This is how the effects of meetings with others can impact on the emotional state of the person and either add to the disability of the person by undermining skills and causing feelings of ill-being or reduce the disability by creating an environment that is empowering to the person and nurtures well-being.

A person-centred philosophy therefore recognizes the uniqueness of the person more than his or her impairment. However, all of the factors that combine within the person need to be understood so that disability is minimised or avoided. Relationships are felt to be at the heart of person-centred philosophy and positive contacts with others can ensure the well-being of people with dementia, regardless of the level of impairment.

Well-being can be described as the state of having a sense of hope, agency, self-confidence and self-esteem. Hope in this way refers to a sense of expectation of positive experiences. Agency refers to a sense of having an impact on the surrounding environment and of being able to make things happen. Self-confidence refers to the feeling of assurance in one's own ability. Self-esteem is a feeling of self-worth. The human need for occupation is satisfied when engagement in it also nurtures these states of well-being.

The Cognitive Disability Model

Cognition is the process by which we think and understand. When a person has a cognitive impairment it may have one or more of several possible causes – illness, trauma, congenital differences, emotional stress – but in all cases there is damage to the nerve and brain tissue, most commonly in the higher brain. This damage causes cognitive impairments of judgement, reasoning, thinking and planning which in turn can lead to disability such as dementia or learning disability. This will be the case if the physical and social environment is disempowering rather than compensating the person for their impairment or enabling him or her to adapt.

The Cognitive Disability Model (CDM) is a model whose clinical application is grounded in occupational therapy. Claudia K. Allen, an American occupational therapist, developed the CDM during her observations of clients with psychiatric disorders. The original theoretical base was influenced by Piaget's theory that cognitive development is a stage process (Piaget 1952). The cognitive model proposed by Piaget looks at the processes of human memory, and puts great emphasis on aspects of being that require highly developed mental skills, but gives little consideration to feelings, emotions and relationships. Allen's later work has developed the theoretical base to include the work of Soviet psychologist Vygotsky, who proposed that human development is a social process involving close interactions between the child and its parents, and later its peers and teachers (Vygotsky 1978).

Allen's description of cognitive disability, based on these earlier theoretical bases, proposes that 'a restriction in voluntary motor action originating in the physical and chemical structures of the brain will produce observable limitations in routine task behaviour' (Allen 1985). Therefore, observing an individual's ability to carry out tasks can indicate damage to those structures. This is because the cognitive processes driving the motor actions in order for the task to be carried out are impaired.

Allen organised this evidence of cognitive impairment into six levels, using descriptions of how an individual attends to the environment, sensory cues and objects. These cognitive levels, that measure a person's ability to function, are based on the stages of development proposed by Piaget. By identifying the cognitive disability of an individual, occupational therapists can also identify his or her remaining abilities. The occupational therapist's role is then to design and test activity environments that utilise these abilities, and to instruct others in maintaining those environments.

The Pool Activity Level (PAL) Instrument takes the information from Allen's Cognitive Disability Model and presents it in a form that is accessible to those without an occupational therapy qualification. It provides the user with a self-interpreting assessment in the form of guides for creating and maintaining facilitating environments. The PAL further develops Allen's more recent attention to the importance of social connections in occupational performance, building on Vygotsky's insights into the importance of providing appropriate assistance and support to the individual while he or she engages in an activity. The PAL Instrument also combines the Cognitive Disability Model with the Socio-psychological Model by focusing the user on the biography of the individual and using this information as a guide to facilitating activities that are meaningful to him or her.

REFERENCES

Allen, C.K. (1985) *Occupational Therapy for Psychiatric Diseases: Measurement and Management of Cognitive Disabilities*. Boston: Little, Brown.

Atkinson, R.L., Atkinson, R.C. and Hilgard E.R. (1983) *Introduction to Psychology 96–99* New York: Harcourt Brace Jonavich (International Edition).

Kitwood, T. (1993) 'Discover the Person, not the Disease.' *Journal of Dementia Care 1*, 1, 16–17.

Piaget, J. (1952) *The Origins of Intelligence in Children*. New York: International Universities Press.

Vygotsky, L.S. (1978) *The Development of Higher Psychological Processes*. Boston: Harvard University Press.

2 The Four Activity Levels

Completing the Pool Activity Level (PAL) Checklist enables care givers to recognize the ability of a person with cognitive impairment to engage in activity. Any individual who knows the person well, by considering how he or she generally functions when carrying out activities, particularly those involving other people, can complete it. These observations should have been made in several situations over a period of one week. If the person lives in a group setting, such as a retirement home, the observations may need to be a compilation from all involved care givers. In this way the variation of abilities and disabilities which can occur in an individual over a period of time is taken into account, and an Occupational Profile can be made. The Occupational Profile gives an overview of the way in which a person best engages in activities and how to create a facilitating environment.

Because there are many factors affecting an individual's ability to engage in an activity – cognitive integrity, the meaningfulness of the task, the familiarity of the environment, the support of others – it is likely that an individual will reveal a variation in his or her level of ability in different activities. The PAL Instrument acknowledges the importance of this and provides the opportunity to create an Individual Action Plan that allows for a varying degree of support in some of the personal activities of daily living.

The PAL is organised into four activity levels: planned, exploratory, sensory and reflex.

Planned Activity Level

At a planned activity level the person can work towards completing a task but may not be able to solve any problems that arise while in the process. He or she will be able to look in obvious places for equipment needed but may not be able to search beyond the usual places. A care giver assisting someone at this level will need to keep his or her sentences short and avoid using words like 'and' or 'but' which tend to be used to link two sentences together into a more complex one. Care givers will also need to stand by to help solve any problems should they arise. People functioning at a planned activity level are able to carry out tasks that achieve a tangible result.

Exploratory Activity Level

At an exploratory activity level the person can carry out very familiar tasks in familiar surroundings. However, at this level people are more concerned with the effect of doing the activity than in the consequence and may not have an end result in mind. Therefore a creative and spontaneous approach by care givers to tasks is helpful. If an activity involves more than two or three tasks, a person at this level will need help in breaking the activity into manageable chunks. Directions need to be made very simple and the use of memory aids such as task lists, calendars and labelling of frequently used items can be very helpful.

Sensory Activity Level

At a sensory activity level the person may not have many thoughts or ideas about carrying out an activity; he or she is mainly concerned with the sensation and with moving his or her body in response to those sensations. People at this level can be guided to carry out single-step tasks such as sweeping or winding wool. More complex activities can only be carried out when directed one step at a time. Therefore care givers need to ensure that the person at this activity level has the opportunity to experience a wide variety of sensations and to carry out one-step tasks. Directions to maximize this opportunity need to be kept very simple and to be reinforced by demonstrating the action required.

Reflex Activity Level

A person at a reflex activity level may not be aware of the surrounding environment or even of his or her own body. He or she is living in a subliminal or subconscious state where movement is a reflex response to a stimulus. Therefore people wishing to enter into this person's consciousness need to use direct sensory stimulation. By using direct stimulation the person's self-awareness can be raised. A person at this level may have difficulty in organising more than one sensation being experienced at the same time.

Excessive or multiple stimuli can cause distress; therefore crowds, loud noises and background clamour should be avoided. Activities at this level should focus on introducing a single sensation to the person. A care giver interacting with a person at a reflex level needs to use all his or her communication skills to enter into the world of a person at this level. Language skills tend to play only a minor role at this level and directions should be kept to single-word commands, although the use of facial expression and of a warm and reassuring tone and volume can be vital in establishing a communication channel.

3 Life History Work

The Importance of Gathering a Life History

Life history work is now recognized as 'an important development that should become a major influence in care planning' (Holden and Woods 1995, p.34).

Life history differs from life review in that it does not require an evaluation of the information that is gathered. Whereas life review is a therapeutic approach to resolving past problems, life history work is not directly aimed at changing a person's view of himself or herself, but rather at care givers who are encouraged to recognize the whole person in the context of their lifespan. The factual account of an individual's life history builds up a full picture of the person. This perspective should assist care givers in their interactions with the person and in planning activities that relate to the person's interests and experiences. The result of this individualized care plan is to recognize the uniqueness of the person and potentially to make a significant change in the quality of his or her life. The purpose of a personal history profile is to enable carers to recognize the person as a unique individual and not to see only the person's disability.

The PAL Instrument Personal History Profile is a method that uses subheadings to guide the user when gathering relevant information. By finding out about all that the person has experienced it is possible to have a better understanding of the person's behaviour now. It also gives care workers, who may not know the person well, topics of conversation that will have meaning for the person.

Putting together the profile should be an enjoyable project that the person with cognitive impairment, relatives and care workers can join together in, encouraging social interaction and reminiscence. The information gained from the personal history profile informs the PAL Activity Profile by guiding activity selection.

Guidelines for Gathering Life History Information Using the Pool Activity Level (PAL) Personal History Profile

The questions in the profile are very general, designed to cater for all people regardless of age or sex. Some questions may be irrelevant, and these should be ignored. If the person is being cared for in a home or hospital or is attending a day centre it may be possible to ask family members to complete the whole form with the person at home. For others, completion of the profile may be spread out over a period of weeks, as more information is revealed. The profile is therefore not an assessment but a means of recording useful information in a systematic way.

Any photographs that are available can be added to the profile. It is helpful to write on the reverse: the person's name; who is in the photograph, and where and when it was taken. Some relatives may be worried about the photographs getting lost or damaged. In these cases, the photographs can be photocopied and the originals kept safe.

A sample of a completed profile is included for information.

Reference

Holden, U. and Woods, R.T. (1995) *Positive Approaches to Dementia Care*. Edinburgh: Churchill Livingstone.

Pool Activity Level (PAL) Personal History Profile

What is your name?	**When were you born?**
Elsie Jones	*10 November 1912*

Childhood

Where were you born?	*Leeds, West Riding of Yorkshire*
What are your family members' names?	*Thomas and Molly Charlton (parents)* *Harry (older brother)*
What were your family members' occupations?	*Sweet-shop owners (parents)* *Tram driver (Harry) but killed in Second World War*
Where did you live?	*Headingley, Leeds*
Which schools did you attend?	*Leeds Girls School*
What was your favourite subject?	*English and Sewing*
Did you have any family pets? What were their names?	*Cats: Charlie/Smudge*

Adolescence

When did you leave school?	*Age 14*
Where did you work?	*Parents' shop, then went to clothing factory, then opened own shop in York in 1952*
What did you do at work?	*Machinist at factory then owned dress shop*
Did you have any special training?	*Can't remember*
What special memories do you have of work days?	*Day trips in summer. Friend, Mary, machined across her finger*
Did you do National Service?	*No*

Adulthood

Do/did you have a partner? Partner's name/occupation?	*Sidney, bank clerk*
Where and when did you meet?	*At a dance in Leeds*
Where and when did you marry?	*5th May 1932 at Headingley Church*
What did you wear? What flowers did you have?	*Cream dress and roses*
Where did you go on honeymoon?	*Scarborough*
Where did you live?	*Leeds, moved to York when Sidney promoted*
Any children – what are their names?	*Shirley, March 1933*
Any grandchildren – what are their names?	*Susan, 1956 and Michael, 1958*
Did you have any special friends? What are their names?	*Barbara*
When and where did you meet? Are they still in touch?	*Factory, see each other sometimes*
Did you have any pets? What were their names?	*Cats, latest one, Susie, is 19 years old*

Retirement

When did you retire?	*1972 age 60. Sidney retired from bank 1979*
What were you looking forward to most?	*Gardening together, touring, visiting family*
What were your hobbies and interests?	*Used to sew and read a lot but stopped when eyes got bad*
What were the biggest changes for you?	*Shirley moving away to London when she married*

Likes and dislikes

What do you enjoy doing now?	*Like to listen to big band music, and to story tapes. Quizzes on the television*
What do you like to read?	*Thrillers, Agatha Christie*
What is your favourite colour?	*Yellow*
What kind of music do you like?	*Big band, Nat King Cole*
What are your favourite foods and drinks?	*Roast meals, chocolate, sherry*
Is there anything that you definitely do not like to do?	*Bingo*

How you like to do things

Do you have any special routines to your day?	*Main meal at lunch time, bath before bed and hot chocolate in bed to settle me*
What time do you like to get up in the morning? And go to bed at night?	*Get up at 9, go to bed after 10 o'clock news*
Do you want people to help you with anything?	*Doing up fastenings and getting in and out of the bath*
Do you want people to leave you to do anything on your own?	*Having a bath, getting dressed except for fastenings*
How do you like people to address you?	*Elsie*
What are you good at?	*Quizzes*
Is there anything else you would like to tell us about you?	*No*

4 PAL Checklist Case Studies

CASE STUDY 1

John is a retired school headmaster who lives with his wife. He is a very precise man who enjoys propagating plants and stamp collecting. Six months ago John went to his GP because he was worried about his increasingly poor memory. The GP diagnosed Alzheimer's disease. This is affecting John's ability to remember the names of friends, plants and stamps in his collection, and he finds this frustrating and embarrassing. His wife is worried that this will lower John's confidence when out and will affect their weekly outings to local restaurants. Although he is able to select cutlery appropriately, he has become less socially outgoing and does not chat to the waiters as he used to.

Although John does have memory problems and is now not paying so much attention to the finer details and finishing touches in his hobbies, he still enjoys being involved in his hobbies with his wife's help.

When John is at ease with others, he is able to start conversations and enjoys discussing topics that he has noticed in the newspaper. Only people close to him realise that he has any disability, and only last week John enjoyed an afternoon with two close friends when they all successfully constructed and painted a new garden shed. There was one moment when he had difficulty with aligning the hinges on the door and could not solve the problem, but one of the others stepped in to help and John was able to carry on with another part of the project.

John is also able to use his own initiative to carry out most everyday tasks. Although his wife has to remind him to have a wash and to shave, John is able to choose what to wear and to get dressed independently.

John and his wife are keen to plan ways of continuing his independence for as long as possible. When the Pool Activity Level (PAL) Checklist is completed for John it reveals that he is able to carry out activities at a planned level. It is now possible to use this information to help John to use his remaining abilities and to compensate for his disabilities.

Pool Activity Level (PAL) Checklist

Name: Date: Outcome:

John Porter   **1st March 2002**   **Planned**

Completing the checklist: for each activity, the statements refer to a different level of ability. Thinking of the last two weeks, tick the statement that represents the person's ability in each activity. There should be only one tick for each activity. If in doubt about which statement to tick, choose the level of ability which represents the person's average performance over the last two weeks. Make sure you tick one statement for each of the activities.

1. Bathing/Washing

- Can bathe/wash independently, sometimes with a little help to start   P: ☑

- Needs soap put on flannel and one-step-at-a-time directions to wash   E: ☐

- Mainly relies on others but will wipe own face and hands if encouraged   S: ☐

- Totally dependent and needs full assistance to wash or bathe   R: ☐

2. Getting dressed

- Plans what to wear, selects own clothing from cupboards; dresses in correct order   P: ☑

- Needs help to plan what to wear but recognizes items and how to wear them; needs help with order of dressing   E: ☐

- Needs help to plan, and with order of, dressing, but can carry out small tasks if someone directs each step   S: ☐

- Totally dependent on someone to plan, sequence and complete dressing; may move limbs to assist   R: ☐

3. Eating

- Eats independently and appropriately using the correct cutlery   P: ☑

- Eats using a spoon and/or needs food to be cut up into small pieces   E: ☐

- Only uses fingers to eat food   S: ☐

- Relies on others to be fed   R: ☐

4. Contact with others

- Initiates social contact and responds to the needs of others   P: ☑

- Aware of others and will seek interaction, but may be more concerned with own needs   E: ☐

- Aware of others but waits for others to make the first social contact   S: ☐

- May not show an awareness of the presence of others unless in direct physical contact   R: ☐

5. Groupwork skills

- Engages with others in a group activity, can take turns with the activity/tools   P: ☑

- Occasionally engages with others in a group, moving in and out of the group at whim   E: ☐

- Aware of others in the group and will work alongside others although tends to focus on own activity   S: ☐

- Does not show awareness of others in the group unless close one-to-one attention is experienced   R: ☐

6. Communication skills

- Is aware of appropriate interaction, can chat coherently and is able to use complex language skills — P: ☑

- Body language may be inappropriate and may not always be coherent, but can use simple language skills — E: ☐

- Responses to verbal interaction may be mainly through body language; comprehension is limited — S: ☐

- Can only respond to direct physical contact from others through touch, eye contact or facial expression — R: ☐

7. Practical activities (craft, domestic chores, gardening)

- Can plan to carry out an activity, hold the goal in mind and work through a familiar sequence; may need help solving problems — P: ☑

- More interested in the making or doing than in the end result, needs prompting to remember purpose, can get distracted — E: ☐

- Activities need to broken be down and presented one step at a time; multisensory stimulation can help to hold the attention — S: ☐

- Unable to 'do' activities, but responds to the close contact of others and experiencing physical sensations — R: ☐

8. Use of objects

- Plans to use and looks for objects that are not visible; may struggle if objects are not in usual/familiar places (i.e. toiletries in a cupboard below washbasin) — P: ☑

- Selects objects appropriately only if in view (i.e. toiletries on a shelf next to washbasin) — E: ☐

- Randomly uses objects as chances upon them; may use inappropriately   S: ☐

- May grip objects when placed in the hand but will not attempt to use them   R: ☐

9. Looking at a newspaper/magazine

- Comprehends and shows interest in the content, turns the pages and looks at headlines and pictures   P: ☑

- Turns the pages randomly, only attending to items pointed out by others   E: ☐

- Will hold and may feel the paper, but will not turn the pages unless directed and will not show interest in the content   S: ☐

- May grip the paper if it is placed in the hand but may not be able to release grip; or may not take hold of the paper   R: ☐

Select the appropriate PAL Profile to act as a general guide to engaging with the person in a variety of activities.

Complete a PAL Individual Action Plan to act as a specific guide to facilitating personal activities.

	Planned	Exploratory	Sensory	Reflex
TOTAL:	9	0	0	0

CASE STUDY 2

Elsie is a retired business woman who owned her own dress shop. Her family have old photographs showing that Elsie was a very well-groomed woman, but sadly she now struggles to dress herself. Elsie is determined to dress herself, but she often looks dishevelled, with petticoats hanging under the hemline of her dress or put on top of her dress, and her hair untidy. Elsie shows that she is aware of her appearance and is often seen tugging at her dress to pull it over the petticoat and smoothing down her hair with her hands.

Elsie has vascular disease and she lives with her daughter and family. They are asking for advice about how they can help Elsie to look smart again without taking away her independence and doing everything for her. Her daughter explains that Elsie relies on her to give her a wash, although she can wipe her face when the soaped cloth is passed to her. She is able to eat her meals using a spoon but struggles to use a knife and fork.

Elsie's family are also concerned that she tries to help with chores but gives up when she cannot find things, and that she tends to blame others, saying someone has not put them away in the right place. For example, Elsie recently became very cross with her granddaughter and accused her of taking her make-up bag, which had actually been tidied away into the top drawer of Elsie's dressing-table.

Also, if something else attracts Elsie's attention, she will leave tasks unfinished. This causes a great deal of untidiness in the home. Elsie was a very sociable lady but has recently become more withdrawn, although she does respond very positively when people draw her out. She enjoys chatting to her grandchildren when the conversation is about simple and familiar events, although she tends to switch off if more complex topics are discussed. Megan, one of

Elsie's granddaughters, likes to sit and look at *Woman and Home* magazine with her, although Elsie tends only to look at articles when Megan points them out.

Elsie enjoys the social and craft activities at the local day centre which she attends once a week, but does not always stay in the groups, preferring to take a walk every so often and return to the group now and again.

When the Pool Activity Level (PAL) Checklist is completed for Elsie it reveals that, in general, she is able to carry out activities at an exploratory level. It is now possible to use this information in the Activity Profile to help Elsie to use her remaining abilities and to compensate for her disabilities. Elsie has differing levels of abilities for different activities. It is therefore also possible to create an Individual Action Plan that recognizes these differences.

Pool Activity Level (PAL) Checklist

Name:
Elsie Jones

Date:
1st March 2002

Outcome:
Exploratory

Completing the checklist: for each activity, the statements refer to a different level of ability. Thinking of the last two weeks, tick the statement that represents the person's ability in each activity. There should be only one tick for each activity. If in doubt about which statement to tick, choose the level of ability which represents their average performance over the last two weeks. Make sure you tick one statement for each of the activities.

1. Bathing/Washing

- Can bathe/wash independently, sometimes with a little help to start   P: ☐

- Needs soap put on flannel and one-step-at-a-time directions to wash   E: ☐

- Mainly relies on others but will wipe own face and hands if encouraged   S: ☑

- Totally dependent and needs full assistance to wash or bathe   R: ☐

2. Getting dressed

- Plans what to wear, selects own clothing from cupboards, dresses in correct order   P: ☐

- Needs help to plan what to wear but recognizes items and how to wear them; needs help with order of dressing   E: ☑

- Needs help to plan, and with order of, dressing, but can carry out small tasks if someone directs each step   S: ☐

- Totally dependent on someone to plan, sequence and complete dressing; may move limbs to assist   R: ☐

3. Eating

- Eats independently and appropriately using the correct cutlery   P: ☐

- Eats using a spoon and/or needs food to be cut up into small pieces   E: ☑

- Only uses fingers to eat food   S: ☐

- Relies on others to be fed   R: ☐

4. Contact with others

- Initiates social contact and responds to the needs of others   P: ☐

- Aware of others and will seek interaction, but may be more concerned with own needs   E: ☐

- Aware of others but waits for others to make the first social contact   S: ☑

- May not show an awareness of the presence of others unless in direct physical contact   R: ☐

5. Groupwork skills

- Engages with others in a group activity, can take turns with the activity/tools   P: ☐

- Occasionally engages with others in a group, moving in and out of the group at whim   E: ☑

- Aware of others in the group and will work alongside others although tends to focus on own activity   S: ☐

- Does not show awareness of others in the group unless close one-to-one attention is experienced   R: ☐

6. Communication skills

- Is aware of appropriate interaction, can chat coherently and is able to use complex language skills **P:** ☐

- Body language may be inappropriate and may not always be coherent, but can use simple language skills **E:** ☑

- Responses to verbal interaction may be mainly through body language; comprehension is limited **S:** ☐

- Can only respond to direct physical contact from others through touch, eye contact or facial expression **R:** ☐

7. Practical activities (craft, domestic chores, gardening)

- Can plan to carry out an activity, hold the goal in mind and work through a familiar sequence; may need help solving problems **P:** ☐

- More interested in the making or doing than in the end result, needs prompting to remember purpose, can get distracted **E:** ☑

- Activities need to be broken down and presented one step at a time; multisensory stimulation can help to hold the attention **S:** ☐

- Unable to 'do' activities, but responds to the close contact of others and experiencing physical sensations **R:** ☐

8. Use of objects

- Plans to use and looks for objects that are not visible; may struggle if objects are not in usual/familiar places (i.e. toiletries in a cupboard below washbasin) **P:** ☐

- Selects objects appropriately only if in view (i.e. toiletries on a shelf next to washbasin) **E:** ☑

- Randomly uses objects as chances upon them; may use inappropriately   S: ☐

- May grip objects when placed in the hand but will not attempt to use them   R: ☐

9. Looking at a newspaper/magazine

- Comprehends and shows interest in the content, turns the pages and looks at headlines and pictures   P: ☐

- Turns the pages randomly, only attending to items pointed out by others   E: ☑

- Will hold and may feel the paper, but will not turn the pages unless directed and will not show interest in the content   S: ☐

- May grip the paper if it is placed in the hand but may not be able to release grip; or may not take hold of the paper   R: ☐

Select the appropriate PAL Profile to act as a general guide to engaging with the person in a variety of activities

Complete a PAL Individual Action Plan to act as a specific guide to facilitating personal activities

	Planned	Exploratory	Sensory	Reflex
TOTAL:	0	7	2	0

CASE STUDY 3

George is a 45-year-old man with learning disability and early onset Alzheimer's disease. He lives in a small-group-living home but he is beginning to rely increasingly on the support workers for all his personal care needs. George is only able to carry out tasks if the support worker guides him through the steps involved. When George is getting dressed, he needs to be offered clothing items, one at a time, and is then able to put on some items if someone talks him through the task. When George has a bath, he relies on the support worker to do everything, only wiping his face and hands with the cloth with the support worker's encouragement.

George used to be a very caring and outgoing person, but now, although he watches the other residents, he does not make the first move to interact with them. When George's friends seek him out he responds readily, although his understanding of their conversation seems limited and his response is mainly a big smile and head nodding rather than with words. George's greatest enjoyment seems to be his mealtimes, and when seated with his friends, he will laugh when he hears them laughing. However, most of his attention is focused on his meal which he eats, using his hands, with great relish.

George used to spend his evenings playing pool with his friends, but this has become difficult because he does not follow the rules of the game and will walk off with the cue. This causes arguments, and George began to spend more time alone, pacing the rooms and picking up items belonging to other residents. When the support workers noticed this, they began to spend more time strolling with him and encouraging him to pick up items that were not contentious. The support workers have noticed that George likes to feel the objects he picks up and that he is drawn to ones with soft textures. They have begun to spend individual time with George, but although they offer to look at the newspaper with him, he seems more interested in the feel of the paper than the content. George does show that he enjoys sitting, holding hands, while they listen together to his favourite music.

Pool Activity Level (PAL) Checklist

Name: **George Owen**

Date: **1st March 2002**

Outcome: **Sensory**

Completing the checklist: for each activity, the statements refer to a different level of ability. Thinking of the last two weeks, tick the statement that represents the person's ability in each activity. There should be only one tick for each activity. If in doubt about which statement to tick, choose the level of ability which represents their average performance over the last two weeks. Make sure you tick one statement for each of the activities.

1. Bathing/Washing

- Can bathe/wash independently, sometimes with a little help to start P: ☐

- Needs soap put on flannel and one-step-at-a-time directions to wash E: ☐

- Mainly relies on others but will wipe own face and hands if encouraged S: ☑

- Totally dependent and needs full assistance to wash or bathe R: ☐

2. Getting dressed

- Plans what to wear, selects own clothing from cupboards; dresses in correct order P: ☐

- Needs help to plan what to wear but recognizes items and how to wear them; needs help with order of dressing E: ☐

- Needs help to plan, and with order of, dressing, but can carry out small tasks if someone directs each step S: ☑

- Totally dependent on someone to plan, sequence and complete dressing; may move limbs to assist R: ☐

3. Eating

- Eats independently and appropriately using the correct cutlery P: ☐

- Eats using a spoon and/or needs food to be cut up into small pieces E: ☐

- Only uses fingers to eat food S: ☑

- Relies on others to be fed R: ☐

4. Contact with others

- Initiates social contact and responds to the needs of others P: ☐

- Aware of others and will seek interaction, but may be more concerned with own needs E: ☐

- Aware of others but waits for others to make the first social contact S: ☑

- May not show an awareness of the presence of others unless in direct physical contact R: ☐

5. Groupwork skills

- Engages with others in a group activity, can take turns with the activity/tools P: ☐

- Occasionally engages with others in a group, moving in and out of the group at whim E: ☐

- Aware of others in the group and will work alongside others although tends to focus on own activity S: ☑

- Does not show awareness of others in the group unless close one-to-one attention is experienced R: ☐

6. Communication skills

- Is aware of appropriate interaction, can chat coherently and is able to use complex language skills   P: ☐

- Body language may be inappropriate and may not always be coherent, but can use simple language skills   E: ☐

- Responses to verbal interaction may be mainly through body language; comprehension is limited   S: ☑

- Can only respond to direct physical contact from others through touch, eye contact or facial expression   R: ☐

7. Practical activities (craft, domestic chores, gardening)

- Can plan to carry out an activity, hold the goal in mind and work through a familiar sequence; may need help solving problems   P: ☐

- More interested in the making or doing than in the end result, needs prompting to remember purpose, can get distracted   E: ☐

- Activities need to be broken down and presented one step at a time; multisensory stimulation can help to hold the attention   S: ☑

- Unable to 'do' activities, but responds to the close contact of others and experiencing physical sensations   R: ☐

8. Use of objects

- Plans to use and looks for objects that are not visible; may struggle if objects are not in usual/familiar places (i.e. toiletries in a cupboard below washbasin)   P: ☐

- Selects objects appropriately only if in view (i.e. toiletries on a shelf next to washbasin)   E: ☐

- Randomly uses objects as chances upon them; may use inappropriately   S: ☑

- May grip objects when placed in the hand but will not attempt to use them   R: ☐

9. Looking at a newspaper/magazine

- Comprehends and shows interest in the content, turns the pages and looks at headlines and pictures   P: ☐

- Turns the pages randomly, only attending to items pointed out by others   E: ☐

- Will hold and may feel the paper, but will not turn the pages unless directed and will not show interest in the content   S: ☑

- May grip the paper if it is placed in the hand but may not be able to release grip; or may not take hold of the paper   R: ☐

Select the appropriate PAL Profile to act as a general guide to engaging with the person in a variety of activities

Complete a PAL Individual Action Plan to act as a specific guide to facilitating personal activities

	Planned	Exploratory	Sensory	Reflex
TOTAL:	0	0	9	0

CASE STUDY 4

Gertie lives on a long-stay hospital ward. She has severe dementia caused by a combination of Alzheimer's disease and vascular disease that has resulted in her experiencing a series of strokes. Gertie relies on the nursing staff for all of her care needs. Gertie does not seem to understand anything that is said to her and most of her contact with others is with people who come up close to her, when she will screw up the muscles of her face and gaze into their eyes. The nursing staff enable her to sit in the group singing activities, and she does become more animated when the music is playing, although she does not seem to be aware of the other group members unless those nearest to her are holding her hands. Gertie will grasp firmly anything that is placed into the palm of her hands and sometimes she has trouble letting go again.

Gertie loves to see children and animals, and will make crooning noises when they visit the ward. She dislikes sudden loud noises and will shout angrily if they disturb her. Gertie used to work in a flower shop and she still loves to look at, and smell, flowers when they are brought to her.

The nursing staff want to help Gertie to engage with her surroundings as much as she can.

Pool Activity Level (PAL) Checklist

Name: Date: Outcome:

Gertie Lawson   **1st March 2002**   **Sensory**

Completing the checklist: for each activity, the statements refer to a different level of ability. Thinking of the last two weeks, tick the statement that represents the person's ability in each activity. There should be only one tick for each activity. If in doubt about which statement to tick, choose the level of ability which represents their average performance over the last two weeks. Make sure you tick one statement for each of the activities.

1. Bathing/Washing

- Can bathe/wash independently, sometimes
  with a little help to start   P: ☐

- Needs soap put on flannel and one-step-at-a-time
  directions to wash   E: ☐

- Mainly relies on others but will wipe own face
  and hands if encouraged   S: ☐

- Totally dependent and needs full assistance
  to wash or bathe   R: ☑

2. Getting dressed

- Plans what to wear, selects own clothing from cupboards;
  dresses in correct order   P: ☐

- Needs help to plan what to wear but recognizes items
  and how to wear them; needs help with order of dressing   E: ☐

- Needs help to plan, and with order of, dressing,
  but can carry out small tasks if someone directs each step   S: ☐

- Totally dependent on someone to plan, sequence
  and complete dressing; may move limbs to assist   R: ☑

3. Eating

- Eats independently and appropriately using the correct cutlery   P: ☐

- Eats using a spoon and/or needs food to be cut up into small pieces   E: ☐

- Only uses fingers to eat food   S: ☐

- Relies on others to be fed   R: ☑

4. Contact with others

- Initiates social contact and responds to the needs of others   P: ☐

- Aware of others and will seek interaction, but may be more concerned with own needs   E: ☐

- Aware of others but waits for others to make the first social contact   S: ☐

- May not show an awareness of the presence of others unless in direct physical contact   R: ☑

5. Groupwork skills

- Engages with others in a group activity, can take turns with the activity/tools   P: ☐

- Occasionally engages with others in a group, moving in and out of the group at whim   E: ☐

- Aware of others in the group and will work alongside others although tends to focus on own activity   S: ☐

- Does not show awareness of others in the group unless close one-to-one attention is experienced   R: ☑

6. Communication skills

- Is aware of appropriate interaction, can chat coherently and is able to use complex language skills   P: ☐

- Body language may be inappropriate and may not always be coherent, but can use simple language skills   E: ☐

- Responses to verbal interaction may be mainly through body language; comprehension is limited   S: ☐

- Can only respond to direct physical contact from others through touch, eye contact or facial expression   R: ☑

7. Practical activities (craft, domestic chores, gardening)

- Can plan to carry out an activity, hold the goal in mind and work through a familiar sequence; may need help solving problems   P: ☐

- More interested in the making or doing than in the end result, needs prompting to remember purpose, can get distracted   E: ☐

- Activities need to be broken down and presented one step at a time; multisensory stimulation can help to hold the attention   S: ☐

- Unable to 'do' activities, but responds to the close contact of others and experiencing physical sensations   R: ☑

8. Use of objects

- Plans to use and looks for objects that are not visible; may struggle if objects are not in usual/familiar places (i.e. toiletries in a cupboard below washbasin)   P: ☐

- Selects objects appropriately only if in view (i.e. toiletries on a shelf next to washbasin)   E: ☐

- Randomly uses objects as chances upon them, may use inappropriately   S: ☐

- May grip objects when placed in the hand but will not attempt to use them   R: ☑

9. Looking at a newspaper/magazine

- Comprehends and shows interest in the content, turns the pages and looks at headlines and pictures   P: ☐

- Turns the pages randomly, only attending to items pointed out by others   E: ☐

- Will hold and may feel the paper, but will not turn the pages unless directed and will not show interest in the content   S: ☐

- May grip the paper if it is placed in the hand but may not be able to release grip; or may not take hold of the paper   R: ☑

Select the appropriate PAL Profile to act as a general guide to engaging with the person in a variety of activities

Complete a PAL Individual Action Plan to act as a specific guide to facilitating personal activities

	Planned	Exploratory	Sensory	Reflex
TOTAL:	0	0	0	9

These case studies give examples of how the behaviour of the person can be recorded to identify the level of ability using the PAL Checklist. The user of the PAL Instrument is then prompted to select the appropriate PAL Profile to act as a general guide to engaging with the person in a variety of activities. Including the information gained from the person's Life History Profile enhances this information.

In addition to the general PAL Profile, the user is also able to complete a PAL Individual Action Plan which acts as a specific guide to facilitating personal activities. In three of the case studies, the level of ability in each task on the checklist is the same throughout. Therefore completion of the Individual Action Plan would use the same level of ability information for all three personal care tasks. In Case Study 2, however, the person is functioning at different levels of ability in different tasks. The Individual Action Plan would reflect this by having a record of how to engage the person in the task at the relevant level of ability as revealed by the Checklist. An example of how to complete the Individual Action Plan in these circumstances is given in Chapter 6.

5 Planning Interventions
Completing the Pool Activity Level (PAL) Profile

When a care giver helps a person with cognitive impairment to carry out a task it is important that they do not do too much as this will undermine the person's self-confidence and could result in the person becoming more dependent. Equally, it is important that care givers do not do too little because the well-being of the person will be undermined as he or she struggles to carry out the task. It is useful to plan the best way of helping the person with cognitive impairments to carry out tasks. Staff in residential homes will be familiar with care plans, although these sometimes focus on the tasks to be done rather than on the method of helping the person to carry them out. Although planning care-giving in a person's own home where a family member, for example, is the carer might seem excessive, it is essential in clarifying the most effective way of enabling the person being cared for. Planning in this way also promotes a consistent approach from all care givers whether they are staff, relatives or friends.

The Pool Activity Level (PAL) Profile assists care givers to translate an understanding of the level of ability of the person with cognitive impairment into practical methods of helping him or her to engage in activities. There are four PAL Profiles, one for each activity level. The care giver should select the Profile which is revealed as appropriate following completion of the PAL Checklist. Each Profile describes how to assist the person by positioning objects that are needed to carry out the activity and by giving verbal or physical directions. The objectives and characteristics of activities that are likely to be meaningful to a person at the level of ability are also described in each Profile.

In addition, some information about the person's likely abilities and limitations are given. This can be helpful in aiding the care giver to build on the person's strengths and to compensate for his or her limitations. In the Checklist examples, John is at a 'Planned' level of ability. As the PAL Profile reveals, this means that he can explore different ways of carrying out an activity and can carry out tasks as long as the objects he needs are in their usual place and the end result of the activity is obvious so that he knows what he is working towards and when he has finished. However, John may not be able to solve any problems that arise and, for example, may not be able to look for any objects that he needs to carry out the task if they are not where he expects to find them.

The Profile for Elsie reveals that she can carry out very familiar activities in very familiar environments but may have a problem with those that involve a complex series of stages, such as getting dressed. So although she is completing the task of getting dressed, and wishes to do this alone, she is not able to carry out the steps involved in the correct sequence and therefore the end result is haphazard. Elsie also tends to start tasks but not finish them and this may be because she has difficulty fixing an end result in her mind at the beginning.

The Checklist example for George reveals that he is able to carry out activities at a 'Sensory' level of ability. The profile indicates that, at this level of ability, George is likely to be responding to bodily sensations rather than engaging in the 'doing' of activities. Any activities he is helped to carry out successfully will be those that are simple one-step ones or those that have been broken down into single stages. At this level, George is likely to be limited in his ability to initiate social contact and will be reliant on others making the first move.

Gertie only engages with her surroundings when there is a direct impact on her own senses. She does not actively seek engagement and so is very reliant on others to ensure that she receives opportunities for stimulation and fulfilment. The Profile for Gertie's 'Reflex' level of ability shows that she can respond in a reflex way to direct sensory stimulation and through this she can become more aware of herself and her surroundings. At this level, Gertie may have difficulty attending to, or may become agitated by, complex and multisensory messages.

Completion of the appropriate PAL Profile will guide care givers in presenting all activities that the person may wish to undertake in a way that maximises the opportunity for meaningful engagement. The example Checklists are developed here so that the Profiles may be clarified.

Blank copies of the PAL Instrument, including the Checklist, Profile, Individual Action Plan and the Outcome Sheet can be found at the back of this book. They may be photocopied for your use with the people for whom you care.

Pool Activity Level (PAL) Profile

Name: John Porter   **Date: 1 March 2002**

Planned Activity Level

ABILITIES

Can explore different ways of carrying out an activity

Can work towards completing a task with a tangible result

Can look in obvious places for any equipment

LIMITATIONS

May not be able to solve problems that arise

May not be able to understand complex sentences

May not search beyond the usual places for equipment

METHOD OF ENGAGEMENT

Activity objectives	To enable *John* to take control of the activity and to master the steps involved
Position of objects	Ensure that equipment and materials are in their usual, familiar places
Verbal directions	Explain task using short sentences, avoiding connecting phrases such as 'and', 'but', 'therefore' or 'if'
Demonstrated directions	Show *John* how to avoid possible errors
Working with others	*John* is able to make the first contact and should be encouraged to initiate social contact
Activity characteristics	There is a goal or end product, with a set process, or 'recipe', to achieve it. An element of competition with others is motivating

This shows that John will remain independent for as long as possible, given the nature of his condition, if his surroundings remain constant so that the familiar positioning of items will act as cues for the next stage in a task. John will also be able to carry out less familiar tasks so long as he is made aware of the aim of an activity and the method is made clear. This clarity will help John to feel confident and secure when he is carrying out tasks so that his self-esteem will not be undermined.

Pool Activity Level (PAL) Profile

Name: Elsie Jones   **Date: I March 2002**

Exploratory Activity Level

ABILITIES

Can carry out very familiar tasks in familiar surroundings

Enjoys the experience of doing a task more than the end result

Can carry out more complex tasks if they are broken down into two- to three-step stages

LIMITATIONS

May not have an end result in mind when starts a task

May not recognize when the task is completed

Relies on cues such as diaries, newspapers, lists and labels

METHOD OF ENGAGEMENT

Activity objectives	To enable *Elsie* to experience the sensation of doing the activity rather than focusing on the end result
Position of objects	Ensure that equipment and materials are in the line of vision
Verbal directions	Explain task using short simple sentences. Avoid using connecting phrases such as 'and', 'but' or 'therefore'.
Demonstrated directions	Break the activity into two to three steps at a time
Working with others	Others must approach *Elsie* and make the first contact
Activity characteristics	There is no pressure to perform to a set of rules, or to achieve an end result. There is an element of creativity and spontaneity

This shows that the care giver needs to guide Elsie to carry out any tasks in stages. Elsie wishes to retain her independence in getting dressed and at the same time to return to her previous standard of grooming. The care giver can facilitate this by helping her sort out her wardrobe and drawers so that items are kept together and are labelled. This may help Elsie to select garments appropriately. In addition, Elsie may enjoy the care giver assisting her while she dresses if the focus is on choosing what to wear and looking at the colours, patterns and texture of the clothes. This is likely to have more meaning for Elsie than the actual act of dressing. It will be important that the care giver helps Elsie to make the finishing touches of hair combing, make-up and jewellery. Elsie can be reassured about her appearance by being encouraged to check herself in a mirror.

This information will help Elsie's family to enable Elsie to experience feelings of self-confidence and self-esteem, because she will be aware that her appearance meets her own standards while at the same time her independence has not been taken away: she has been enabled to carry out the dressing task at her own level of ability.

Pool Activity Level (PAL) Profile

Name: George Owen   **Date: I March 2002**

Sensory Activity Level

ABILITIES	LIMITATIONS
Is likely to be responsive to bodily sensations	May not have any conscious plan to carry out a movement to achieve a particular end result
Can be guided to carry out single-step tasks	May be relying on others to make social contact
Can carry out more complex tasks if they are broken down into one step at a time	

METHOD OF ENGAGEMENT

Activity objectives	To enable *George* to experience the effect of the activity on the senses
Position of objects	Ensure that *George* becomes aware of equipment and materials by making bodily contact
Verbal directions	Limit requests to carry out actions to the naming of actions and objects, e.g. 'Lift your arm', 'Hold the brush'
Demonstrated directions	Show *George* the action on the object. Break the activity down into one step at a time
Working with others	Others must approach *George* and make the first contact. Use touch and *George's* name to sustain the social contact
Activity characteristics	The activity is used as an opportunity for a sensory experience. This may be multisensory and repetitive

As we see in George's case study (Chapter 4) George is engaging with his surroundings by enjoying the sensations, particularly of touch. The care givers have recognized the importance of this to George and are providing him with opportunities for interacting with them through the medium of touch.

This Profile will help care givers to realize that it is important for George to enjoy being involved in the process of carrying out the activity rather than in the end result. It will also help them to recognize that, despite his disability, George still has many abilities and that he can do activities which do not involve more than one step. There are many such activities, including sweeping, polishing and wiping surfaces.

When activities are presented to George in this way he is likely to regain his sense of being a part of things in his home and, by his actions, of being able to make things happen.

Pool Activity Level (PAL) Profile

Name: Gertie Lawson   **Date: 1 March 2002**

Reflex Activity Level

ABILITIES

Can make reflex responses to direct sensory stimulation

Can increase awareness of self, and others, by engagement of senses

May respond to social engagement through the use of body language

LIMITATIONS

May be in a subliminal or subconscious state

May have difficulty organizing the multiple sensations that are being experienced

May become agitated in an environment that is over-stimulating

METHOD OF ENGAGEMENT

Activity objectives	To arouse *Gertie* to a conscious awareness of self
Position of objects	Stimulate area of body being targeted, e.g. stroke *Gertie's* arm before placing it in a sleeve
Verbal directions	Limit spoken directions to movement directions, i.e. 'Lift', 'Hold', 'Open'
Demonstrated directions	Guide movements by touching the relevant body part
Working with others	Maintain eye contact, make maximum use of facial expression, gestures and body posture for a nonverbal conversation. Use social actions which can be imitated, e.g. smiling, waving, shaking hands
Activity characteristics	The activity is in response to direct selective sensory stimulation

Gertie's Profile reveals how important it is that others approach her and make contact with her by stimulating her sense of hearing, sight, smell, taste or touch. When this happens, Gertie obviously responds, so planning to make it happen frequently will give Gertie an increased opportunity for engaging with others and her surroundings.

These are examples of how a Pool Activity Level (PAL) Profile can be used to address one aspect of a person's life. Most care givers, though, are concerned with much more than just one task. They want to know how to help the person they care for to undertake a range of activities and thus to maintain a stimulating and fulfilling life.

The Profile describes *how*, in general, to help people with cognitive impairment according to their different levels of ability. The final stage of using the PAL Profile is to work out *what* activities should be provided or encouraged and enter this information in the final box on the Profile form. Chapter 7 describes how to use the information from the Life History Profile to ensure that activities that are meaningful to the person are entered on this form.

Care givers often seek specific guidance in enabling the person they care for to realise his or her potential for carrying out personal care activities such as bathing, dining or dressing. The Pool Activity Level (PAL) Individual Action Plan has been designed to be used in this way so that a person with cognitive impairment is facilitated to carry out a range of personal care tasks using his or her abilities.

Completing the Pool Activity Level (PAL) Individual Action Plan

A person with cognitive impairment will have some cognitive skills that are still intact. These will vary depending on the area of damage in the brain. In any case the ability to carry out tasks does not always rely on the integrity of the brain; familiarity with the task and the task environment, and the type of support the person receives while carrying out the task will either facilitate or undermine the person's ability. It is often apparent that a person does have different levels of ability in different tasks. Completion of the PAL Checklist can be helpful in revealing this. The care giver is guided to note the level of ability of the person in the tasks of dressing, bathing and dining and then to refer to the Individual Action Plan Guidance Notes. These reveal a method for facilitating the person's engagement in each of the three tasks.

Transferring the information from the Guidance Notes on to the Individual Action Plan can be completed in several ways. The user can photocopy the Guidance Notes and then cut them out and stick them on to the Individual Action Plan, or the user may prefer to handwrite the information. If there is access to a computer, the user may transfer the

PAL Instrument on to it and use the cut and paste facility to enter the relevant information on to the Individual Action Plan.

Because social and psychological factors also play an important role in determining an individual's ability to carry out a task, the user is also encouraged to consider these when completing the Individual Action Plan. By referring to the person's Life History Profile, and by observing the person's responses when assisting him or her to carry out a task, it is possible also to pay attention to the person's preferences and to plan to accommodate these.

In the Pool Activity Level (PAL) Checklist examples (Chapter 5) it was revealed that Elsie, in general, is able to carry out activities at an exploratory level. This information was used to complete the Activity Profile to help Elsie to use her remaining abilities and to compensate for her disabilities. It was also noted, though, that Elsie has differing levels of abilities for different activities. It is therefore also possible to create an Individual Action Plan that recognizes these differences.

Pool Activity Level (PAL) Individual Action Plan

Name: Elsie Jones   **Date: 1 March 2002**

Dressing

Favourite garments   Dresses, cardigans

Preferred routine   Dress after breakfast, in bedroom

Grooming likes and dislikes   Does not like hair to be left loose or to wear slides. Wears lipstick and blusher (in top drawer of dressing table)

METHOD: EXPLORATORY ACTIVITY LEVEL

- Encourage discussion about the clothing to be worn for the day: whether it is suitable for the weather or the occasion, whether it is a favourite item and so on.

- Spend time colour-matching items of clothing and select accessories.

- Break down the task into manageable chunks: help lay the clothes out in order, for example, so that underclothing is at the top of the pile.

- Encourage Elsie to check her appearance in the mirror.

Bathing

Favourite toiletries   Lavender bath foam, Palmolive soap, lavender talcum powder

Preferred routine   Bath at 9.30 p.m., then wears nightgown and dressing-gown and has hot chocolate while watching 10 o'clock news before going to bed

Bathing likes and dislikes   Likes bath to be full but not too hot. Prefers to use a sponge for her body and a cloth for her face

METHOD: SENSORY ACTIVITY LEVEL

- Prepare the bathroom and run the bath-water for Elsie.

- Make the bathroom warm and inviting – play music, use scented oils or bubble bath, have candles lit and placed safely out of reach.

- Break down the task into one step at a time and give Elsie simple directions: 'Rub the soap on the cloth, rub your arm, rinse your arm, rub your chest, rinse your chest…'

Dining

Favourite foods   Casseroles, soup, treacle pudding

Preferred routine   Main meal at lunch time, tea at 5 and a light supper at 8.30 before bathing

Dining likes and dislikes   Does not like spicy foods. Prefers small portions and likes food to be cut up

METHOD: EXPLORATORY ACTIVITY LEVEL

- Store cutlery and crockery in view and encourage Elsie to select own tools for dining.

- Offer food using simple choices.

- Create a social atmosphere using, for example, table decorations and music, and promote conversation.

6 Implementing Interventions

Activities

When considering the range of activities in which we engage, it is useful to split them into three main categories: personal care tasks; domestic tasks, such as cleaning, cooking and gardening; and leisure interests. A person with cognitive impairment can be helped to carry out any of these activities using the PAL Profile, and the Individual Action Plan pays particular attention to the personal care activities.

Most care givers find that there is insufficient time for the person they care for to carry out all tasks at his or her own level of ability, particularly when the pace of the person is slowed. For many family care givers, the demands of enabling the person they care for to work through a task can be physically and emotionally exhausting. Attempting to work to one's full potential in all areas of daily life will be equally exhausting to the person with cognitive impairment. For care givers in communal settings, such as residential homes or hospitals, there are often not enough staff to allow this amount of individual time with people.

The solution is to give priority to the activities that have the most importance for the person with cognitive impairment so that he or she is able to do as much as is possible in those aspects, at the same time helping him or her to conserve energy by giving increased assistance in areas that are felt to be of lesser importance. For example, Elsie, who has always paid a lot of attention to her physical appearance, may be enabled to carry out grooming tasks to her full potential, but domestic chores such as making the bed can be done for her. George, who shows great enthusiasm for the social and the dining aspects of mealtimes and has begun to respond to the sensory experiences around him, may prefer to accept assistance with his bathing and dressing needs so that he has more time and energy to enjoy engaging with others through these sensory opportunities.

Care givers who are close relatives or friends will have a wealth of information about the life history and the personality of the person with cognitive impairment. The PAL Life History Profile (Chapter 4) is a useful guide to gathering and recording this type of information and is a valuable starting-point in planning which occupations will be of most interest. If the person is living in a communal setting, the care giver can share this information with the staff so that the most appropriate occupations are offered. If the person lives at home with a care giver, and services such as home care are provided, this information can be also shared with those service providers.

Care givers sometimes feel that it is inappropriate to encourage the person with cognitive impairment to carry out an occupation that cannot be performed at as high a standard as previously. If the person is still interested in the activity, it is likely that he or she will still enjoy the opportunity to carry it out and, if the person is concerned about the standard of the final outcome, by having the activity presented using the guidelines in the PAL Profile the person will be able to engage with the activity in manageable stages. For many people with cognitive impairment, it is not the final end product that is as important as the opportunity to engage in the process of doing the activity. When care givers recognize this they can place less emphasis on what has been achieved in terms of final product than on what has been achieved in terms of experiencing the activity.

The knowledge of a person's interests and familiar routines, together with an understanding of how he or she best carries out activities, can be utilized to ensure occupations are engaged in that are unique to the individual. As the person is provided with opportunities to become meaningfully occupied, it may well be that his or her cognitive and functional ability will improve. Adopting a facilitating approach should help the person's level of ability to be sustained for longer. Even when a person's ability level decreases, as is possible given the nature of some of the conditions causing cognitive impairment, it is unlikely that the person's interests will change. Therefore activities associated with these may continue, using the Action Plan for the new level. For example, John may be helped to engage in gardening activities using the PAL Action Plan at a planned level of ability. In the future, he may lose some of these abilities and it may become appropriate still to present gardening opportunities to him, but to use the PAL Action Plan for an exploratory level of ability that will give guidance on how to continue to facilitate his gardening interest.

It is proposed that it is possible to take any activity that a person is interested in and use the appropriate Action Plan to present it at the right level for that individual.

Examples of some typical activities, which can be presented at either a planned, exploratory, sensory or reflex level, are presented on the next pages. These are intended to give a flavour of how the information in the Action Plan can be translated into everyday practice.

ACTIVITY: GARDENING

Planned Activity Level

- Plan a planting task by looking through seed catalogues and gardening magazines, or by visiting a gardening centre.

- Encourage the person to take charge of getting the equipment off the gardening shelf/trolley and planting the plants out in the garden or tub.

- Hand over the responsibility for watering or weeding (the person may need reminding).

- Encourage the person to clean up after the task is completed and to put away tools in the appropriate places.

Exploratory Activity Level

- Encourage the person to be creative with the planting arrangement and to select unusual containers, and spend time discussing which plants will look attractive in them.

- Arrange a workspace close to where the equipment is on view. Ensure that items are obvious: keep plant labels and the potting compost bag turned towards the person so that the writing and pictures are visible.

- Break down the task into manageable chunks: suggest to the person that he or she uses a trowel or old spoon to fill the tray or bowl with potting compost; when that is accomplished suggest that the plants be placed in the container and, when that is achieved, suggest that the person fills a watering-can and waters the plants.

- Create a social occasion; perhaps use the activity as an opportunity to reminisce about previous gardens or to discuss favourite plants.

Sensory Activity Level

- Prepare a table with the planting equipment.

- Encourage the person to use his or her hands to put the potting compost into the containers. Spend time crumbling it and smoothing it with the fingers.

- Plant scented herbs or lemon geranium. Encourage the person to crush some leaves in his or her fingers and to smell or taste them.

- Enter watering into the person's weekly planner or diary and accompany him or her on this task.

Reflex Activity Level

- Have the person next to you when you carry out the planting task. Ensure that he or she is comfortable and can see what you are doing.

- Keep equipment that is not being used out of the person's line of vision.

- Offer a plant to the person to smell by placing your fingers over theirs and, together, gently crush the plant. Raise the person's hand to his or her face and suggest that they smell the plant.

- Use your body language – smiling and nodding – to reinforce that this is a pleasant experience for you, too.

ACTIVITY: PREPARING A FRUIT SALAD

Planned Activity Level

- Use a recipe card with a picture of the end result.

- Encourage the person to follow the directions on the recipe card to make the fruit juice base for the salad.

- Encourage the person to take charge of cutting the fruit up and arranging it in the bowl.

Exploratory Activity Level

- Use a tin of fruit as a base for the salad so that the juice does not have to be made. Add fresh orange juice to it so that there is sufficient juice. Have a selection of fresh fruit to add to the base.

- Arrange a workplace close to where the equipment is on view. Ensure that items needed are obvious: keep the tin of fruit and the orange juice carton turned so that the labels are visible.

- Encourage the person to be creative about selecting the fruit and the container to be used, and spend time discussing which colours of fruit will look attractive.

- Break down the task into manageable chunks: suggest to the person that he or she opens the tin and empties it into the salad container; when that is accomplished suggest that you will peel the fruit while the person chops it.

- Create a social occasion out of the task: use it as an opportunity to reminisce about family meals or to discuss favourite foods.

Sensory Activity Level

- Prepare the table with an orange, apple, pear and seedless grapes, a container and the cutlery. Open a tin of pineapple to act as a base for the salad.

- Encourage the person to handle each piece of fruit, to feel the texture of the skin and to smell it.

- Break down the task into one step at a time: peel the orange and suggest that the person split the segments while you chop the apple and pear. When this is accomplished, suggest to the person that he or she picks the grapes off the stem and puts them into the container with the rest of the salad.

- When finished, encourage the person to smell and to lick his or her fingers and to enjoy the aroma and the look of the fruit salad.

Reflex Activity Level

- Position the person next to you when you prepare the fruit salad. Ensure that the person is comfortable and can see what you are doing.

- Only have on view the piece of fruit which you are preparing; keep the fruit and equipment that is not in immediate use out of the person's line of vision.

- Place a piece of soft fruit, such as a banana or kiwi fruit, in the person's hand and help him or her to hold it by placing your fingers over theirs. Raise the person's hand to his or her face and encourage them to smell and taste.

- Use your body language – smiling and nodding – to reinforce that this is a pleasant experience for you, too.

7 Seeing Results

Aims and Rationale of the PAL Instrument

The purpose of this guidebook is not simply to encourage readers to embark on a purely academic exercise to find out the level of a person's cognitive disability and the corresponding level of functional ability. The guidebook is intended to enable care givers to enhance the experience of the person with cognitive impairment through an increased understanding of his or her abilities and the provision of appropriately presented occupations. When this occurs there is often an effect on the person's psychological, social and cognitive experience. In other words, the person may not only have enhanced feelings of self-confidence and self-esteem, he or she may also experience a higher level of thinking and reasoning, and of communication with others.

The Person-centred Approach

A person-centred approach is possible because of the close relationship between cognition, feeling and action. It is helpful to view these three states as the points of a triangle, each being separate from, but also interrelating with, the others. For example, low feelings cause every person to think, reason and act less efficiently. Equally, negative thoughts cause low feelings and can stifle the ability to act effectively; and a lack of action can lead to low mood and negative thoughts. A knowledge of this triangle can be used by care givers to raise the level of ability in all three areas by focusing on the two which are the most easily influenced in a person with cognitive impairment: feelings and actions.

This concept is at the heart of a person-centred approach to caring for people with dementia (Kitwood 1990), which is grounded in the theory that dementia is a disability caused not only by neurological impairment but also by a damaging social psychology, undermining interactions with others and a lack of opportunity for engagement in meaningful occupation.

Actions and activities can be used by care givers as a vehicle for interaction. Communication which achieves close contact between the care giver and the person with cognitive impairment will enhance the person's mood. In addition, if the activity or action is facilitated at the right level for the individual, feelings of self-confidence and self-esteem will also be experienced as the person is able to participate successfully. This type of success is not unusual and many care givers report that the person they care for seems at times to improve beyond expectation.

Recording the Results of Activities

Giving real life 'before and after' descriptions is an interesting way for care givers to describe the results of their activity with an individual; but a story in itself may not be sufficient to convince others of the potential for improvement. Hard facts are sometimes needed. That is why it is helpful to keep records that show the progress of the person with cognitive impairment, not only in their actions by recording what they can or cannot do but also in their experiences by recording what they seem to be feeling as portrayed by their behaviour.

The PAL Outcome Sheet

The PAL Outcome Sheet is one simple method using a tick list to record the response of a person to the activity in which they have been engaged. It makes statements of behaviours that are likely to be observed when people are engaging in activities at each of the four activity levels. This helps the care giver to identify easily whether the person responded as expected and whether his or her experience was a positive one. The Checklist can be used to monitor the progress of the person over a period of time, and it can also be used by care givers to monitor their own progress – to determine whether they are getting it right.

Care givers of people in their own home who have cognitive impairment may feel that record keeping is not for them, that it is only necessary for hospitals and homes. But record keeping need not be complex or time consuming and it can have two major impacts on the experience of the people being cared for. First, if care givers from all settings keep records, then they can contribute to research into effective ways of working with people with cognitive impairments. Second, if care givers keep records and are actively seeking improvements in the experience of the person or people they care for, then they are maintaining an attitude of expectation rather than one of acceptance that there is no scope for improvement. The negative culture of assuming an inevitable decline of the person with cognitive impairment where the cause is viewed as progressive, such as in Alzheimer's disease, is now held to be harmful itself – it may become a self-fulfilling prophesy. If care givers and the person being cared for accept this assumption, the person's psychological well-being is undermined and this can adversely affect the person's physical health and functional ability. An expectation that positive care giving can have a healing effect, where the person may improve to a higher level of cognition and ability, will change the whole culture of caring for this group of people.

Reference

Kitwood, T. (1990) 'The dialectics of dementia: With particular reference to Alzheimer's disease.' *Ageing and Society 10*, 177–196.

8 Pool Activity Level (PAL) Instrument

Directions

Completing the PAL Life History Profile

The aim is to gather and record information that will improve opportunities for the person with cognitive impairment to engage in meaningful activity. Completion of the Life History Profile will depend on what sections are relevant, what information is available and what the person wishes to be recorded. It is likely to be an ongoing process rather than a once-only task and can become a meaningful activity for the person in itself.

Completing the PAL Checklist

Consider how the person with cognitive impairment generally functions when carrying out the activities described in the Checklist. If you are unsure, observe the person in the situations over a period of two weeks. If the person lives in a group setting, such as a home, you might need to ask other care givers for their observations, too.

For each activity the statements refer to a different level of ability. Thinking of the last two weeks, tick the statement that represents the person's ability in each activity. There should be only one tick for each activity. If in doubt about which statement to tick, choose the level of ability that represents the person's average performance over the last two weeks. Make sure you tick one statement for each of the activities.

Interpreting the Checklist

People do not fit neatly into boxes, and the PAL Instrument is designed to describe people in simple terms so that it is widely applicable. Add up the number of ticks for each activity level and enter the number in the total box at the end of the Checklist. You should find that there is a majority of ticks at one of the levels. This indicates which Activity Profile to select. If the number of ticks is evenly divided between two activity levels, assume that the person is currently functioning at the lower level of ability for the purpose of selecting the Activity Profile, but ensure that the person has opportunity to move into the higher level of ability.

Completing the Activity Profile

This is a general description of the environment in which the person is likely to best engage in activities. The box at the end of the Activity Profile should be completed by referring to the information gathered and recorded in the Life History Profile. This is how the general nature of the Activity Profile becomes individualised.

Completing the Individual Action Plan

Note the level of ability of the person in the tasks of dressing, bathing and dining that have been revealed on the PAL Checklist and refer to the Individual Action Plan Guidance Notes. These reveal a method for facilitating the person's engagement in each of the three tasks. Enter the methods of facilitating the engagement of the person with cognitive disability on to the relevant section of the Individual Action Plan.

Transferring the information from the Guidance Notes on to the Individual Action Plan can be completed in several ways. The user can photocopy the Guidance Notes and then cut and stick them on to the Individual Action Plan, or the user may prefer to handwrite the information. If there is access to a computer, the user may transfer the PAL Instrument on to it and use the cut and paste facility to enter the relevant information on to the Individual Action Plan.

Completing the Outcome Sheet

Use one column of the Outcome Sheet for each activity engaged in. Enter the date and the type of activity in the appropriate boxes and tick the statements that apply. It can be useful to use one Outcome Sheet for a specific activity so that responses to that activity can be monitored over a period of time. Alternatively, a range of activities can be monitored.

Pool Activity Level (PAL) Personal History Profile

The purpose of a Personal History Profile is to enable carers to recognize the person as a unique individual and not to see only the person's disability. By finding out about all that the person has experienced it is possible to have a better understanding of the person's behaviour now. It also gives care workers, who do not know the person very well, topics of conversation that will have meaning for the person

Putting together the Profile should be an enjoyable project that the person with dementia, relatives and care workers can join in together, encouraging life review and reminiscence. The information gained from the personal history profile informs the PAL Activity Profile by guiding activity selection.

The questions in the Profile are very general, to cater for all people regardless of age or sex. Some questions may be irrelevant, so just ignore these!

If you can include any photographs to add to this profile please write on the reverse:

- person's name

- who is in the photo

- where and when it was taken.

If you are worried about the photographs getting lost or damaged, you could have them photocopied.

Pool Activity Level (PAL) Personal History Profile

What is your name?   **When were you born?**

Childhood

Where were you born?

What are your family members' names?

What were your family members' occupations?

Where did you live?

Which schools did you attend?

What was your favourite subject?

Did you have any family pets? What were their names?

Adolescence

When did you leave school?

Where did you work?

What did you do at work?

Did you have any special training?

What special memories do you have of work days?

Did you do National Service?

Adulthood

Do/did you have a partner?
Partner's name/occupation?

Where and when did you meet?

Where and when did you marry?

What did you wear? What
flowers did you have?

Where did you go on
honeymoon?

Where did you live?

Any children – what are their
names?

Any grandchildren – what are
their names?

Did you have any special friends?
What are their names?

When and where did you meet?
Are they still in touch?

Did you have any pets? What
were their names?

Retirement

When did you retire?

What were you looking
forward to most?

What were your hobbies
and interests?

What were the biggest changes
for you?

Likes and dislikes

What do you enjoy doing now?

What do you like to read?

What is your favourite colour?

What kind of music do you like?

What are your favourite foods and drinks?

Is there anything that you definitely do not like to do?

How you like to do things

Do you have any special routines to your day?

What time do you like to get up in the morning? And go to bed at night?

Do you want people to help you with anything?

Do you want people to leave you to do anything on your own?

How do you like people to address you?

What are you good at?

Is there anything else you would like to tell us about you?

Pool Activity Level (PAL) Checklist

Name: Date: Outcome:

Completing the checklist. For each activity, the statements refer to a different level of ability. Thinking of the last two weeks, tick the statement that represents the person's ability in each activity. There should be only one tick for each activity. If in doubt about which statement to tick, choose the level of ability which represents the person's average performance over the last two weeks. Make sure you tick one statement for each of the activities.

1. Bathing/Washing

- Can bathe/wash independently, sometimes with
  a little help to start   P: ☐

- Needs soap put on flannel and one-step-at-a-time
   directions to wash   E: ☐

- Mainly relies on others but will wipe own face and hands
  if encouraged   S: ☐

- Totally dependent and needs full assistance
  to wash or bathe   R: ☐

2. Getting dressed

- Plans what to wear, selects own clothing from cupboards;
  dresses in correct order   P: ☐

- Needs help to plan what to wear but recognizes items
  and how to wear them; needs help with order of dressing   E: ☐

- Needs help to plan, and with order of, dressing, but can
  carry out small tasks if someone directs each step   S: ☐

- Totally dependent on someone to plan, sequence
  and complete dressing; may move limbs to assist   R: ☐

3. Eating

- Eats independently and appropriately using the correct cutlery   P: ☐

- Eats using a spoon and/or needs food to be cut up into small pieces   E: ☐

- Only uses fingers to eat food   S: ☐

- Relies on others to be fed   R: ☐

4. Contact with others

- Initiates social contact and responds to the needs of others   P: ☐

- Aware of others and will seek interaction, but may be more concerned with own needs   E: ☐

- Aware of others but waits for others to make the first social contact   S: ☐

- May not show an awareness of the presence of others unless in direct physical contact   R: ☐

5. Groupwork skills

- Engages with others in a group activity, can take turns with the activity/tools   P: ☐

- Occasionally engages with others in a group, moving in and out of the group at whim   E: ☐

- Aware of others in the group and will work alongside others although tends to focus on own activity   S: ☐

- Does not show awareness of others in the group unless close one-to-one attention is experienced   R: ☐

6. Communication skills

- Is aware of appropriate interaction, can chat coherently and is able to use complex language skills   P: ☐

- Body language may be inappropriate and may not always be coherent, but can use simple language skills   E: ☐

- Responses to verbal interaction may be mainly through body language; comprehension is limited   S: ☐

- Can only respond to direct physical contact from others through touch, eye contact or facial expression   R: ☐

7. Practical activities (craft, domestic chores, gardening)

- Can plan to carry out an activity, hold the goal in mind and work through a familiar sequence; may need help solving problems   P: ☐

- More interested in the making or doing than in the end result, needs prompting to remember purpose, can get distracted   E: ☐

- Activities need to be broken down and presented one step at a time; multisensory stimulation can help to hold the attention   S: ☐

- Unable to 'do' activities, but responds to the close contact of others and experiencing physical sensations   R: ☐

8. Use of objects

- Plans to use and looks for objects that are not visible; may struggle if objects are not in usual/familiar places (i.e. toiletries in a cupboard below washbasin)   P: ☐

- Selects objects appropriately only if in view (i.e. toiletries on a shelf next to washbasin)   E: ☐

- Randomly uses objects as chances upon them; may use inappropriately   S: ☐

- May grip objects when placed in the hand but will not attempt to use them   R: ☐

9. Looking at a newspaper/magazine

- Comprehends and shows interest in the content, turns the pages and looks at headlines and pictures   P: ☐

- Turns the pages randomly, only attending to items pointed out by others   E: ☐

- Will hold and may feel the paper, but will not turn the pages unless directed and will not show interest in the content   S: ☐

- May grip the paper if it is placed in the hand but may not be able to release grip; or may not take hold of the paper   R: ☐

Select the appropriate PAL Profile to act as a general guide to engaging with the person in a variety of activities.

Complete a PAL Individual Action Plan to act as a specific guide to facilitating personal activities.

	Planned	Exploratory	Sensory	Reflex
TOTAL:				

Pool Activity Level (PAL) Profile

Name: **Date:**

Planned Activity Level

ABILITIES	LIMITATIONS
Can explore different ways of carrying out an activity	May not be able to solve problems that arise
Can work towards completing a task with a tangible result	May not be able to understand complex sentences
Can look in obvious places for any equipment	May not search beyond the usual places for equipment

METHOD OF ENGAGEMENT

Activity objectives	To enable … to take control of the activity and to master the steps involved
Position of objects	Ensure that equipment and materials are in their usual, familiar places
Verbal directions	Explain task using short sentences, avoiding connecting phrases such as 'and', 'but', 'therefore' or 'if'
Demonstrated directions	Show … how to avoid possible errors
Working with others	… is able to make the first contact and should be encouraged to initiate social contact
Activity characteristics	There is a goal or end product, with a set process, or 'recipe', to achieve it. An element of competition with others is motivating

Suitable activities (based on knowledge of the person's life history)

....

....

Pool Activity Level (PAL) Profile

Name: **Date:**

Exploratory Activity Level

ABILITIES

Can carry out very familiar tasks in familiar surroundings

Enjoys the experience of doing a task more than the end result

Can carry out more complex tasks if they are broken down into two- to three-step stages

LIMITATIONS

May not have an end result in mind when starts a task

May not recognize when the task is completed

Relies on cues such as diaries, newspapers, lists and labels

METHOD OF ENGAGEMENT

Activity objectives	To enable … to experience the sensation of doing the activity rather than focusing on the end result
Position of objects	Ensure that equipment and materials are in the line of vision
Verbal directions	Explain task using short simple sentences. Avoid using connecting phrases such as 'and', 'but' or 'therefore'
Demonstrated directions	Break the activity into two to three steps at a time
Working with others	Others must approach … and make the first contact
Activity characteristics	There is no pressure to perform to a set of rules, or to achieve an end result. There is an element of creativity and spontaneity

Suitable activities (based on knowledge of the person's life history)

....

....

Name: **Date:**
Sensory Activity Level

ABILITIES	LIMITATIONS
Is likely to be responding to bodily sensations	May not have any conscious plan to carry out a movement to achieve a particular end result
Can be guided to carry out single step tasks	May be relying on others to make social contact
Can carry out more complex tasks if they are broken down into one step at a time	

METHOD OF ENGAGEMENT

Activity objectives	To enable … to experience the effect of the activity on the senses
Position of objects	Ensure that … becomes aware of equipment and materials by making bodily contact
Verbal directions	Limit requests to carry out actions to the naming of actions and objects, e.g. 'Lift your arm', 'Hold the brush'
Demonstrated directions	Show … the action on the object. Break the activity down into one step at a time
Working with others	Others must approach … and make the first contact. Use touch and … name to sustain the social contact
Activity characteristics	The activity is used as an opportunity for a sensory experience. This may be multisensory and repetitive

Suitable activities (based on knowledge of the person's life history)

....

....

Pool Activity Level (PAL) Profile

Name:
Reflex Activity Level

Date:

ABILITIES

Can make reflex responses to direct sensory stimulation

Can increase awareness of self, and others, by engagement of senses

May respond to social engagement through the use of body language

LIMITATIONS

May be in a subliminal or subconscious state

May have difficulty organizing the multiple sensations that are being experienced

May become agitated in an environment that is over-stimulating

METHOD OF ENGAGEMENT

Activity objectives	To arouse … to a conscious awareness of self
Position of objects	Stimulate area of body being targeted, e.g. stroke … arm before placing it in a sleeve
Verbal directions	Limit spoken directions to movement directions, i.e. 'Lift', 'Hold', 'Open'
Demonstrated directions	Guide movements by touching the relevant body part
Working with others	Maintain eye contact, make maximum use of facial expression, gestures and body posture for a nonverbal conversation. Use social actions which can be imitated, e.g. smiling, waving, shaking hands
Activity characteristics	The activity is in response to direct selective sensory stimulation

Suitable activities (based on knowledge of the person's life history)

....

....

Pool Activity Level (PAL) Individual Action Plan

Name: **Date:**

Dressing

Favourite garments

Preferred routine

Grooming likes and dislikes

METHOD

Bathing

Favourite toiletries

Preferred routine

Bathing likes and dislikes

METHOD

Dining

Favourite foods

Preferred routine

Dining likes and dislikes

METHOD

Pool Activity Level (PAL) Individual Action Plan Guidance Notes

Refer to the level of ability for each task that has been revealed on the **PAL Checklist** and enter the methods for facilitating the engagement of the person with cognitive disability on to the relevant section of the **Individual Action Plan**

Activity: Dressing

PLANNED ACTIVITY LEVEL

- Encourage (the person) to plan what to wear and to select own clothes from the wardrobe.

- Encourage (the person) to put on (his/her) own clothes; be available to assist if required.

- Point out labels on clothing to help orientate the back from the front.

- Encourage (the person) to attend to grooming such as brushing hair, putting on make-up, cleaning shoes.

EXPLORATORY ACTIVITY LEVEL

- Encourage discussion about the clothing to be worn for the day: is it suitable for the weather or the occasion; is it a favourite item?

- Spend time colour-matching items of clothing and select accessories.

- Break down the task into manageable chunks: help lay the clothes out in order so that underclothing is at the top of the pile. If the person wishes to be helped, talk (the person) through the task: 'Put on your underclothes'; 'Now put on your dress and cardigan'.

- Encourage (the person) to check (his/her) appearance in the mirror.

SENSORY ACTIVITY LEVEL

- Offer a simple choice of clothing to be worn.

- Spend a few moments enjoying the sensations of the clothing: feeling the fabric, rubbing the person's finger up and down a zip fastener, or smelling the clean laundry.

- Break down the task into one step at a time: 'Put on your vest'; 'Now put on your pants'; 'Now put on your stockings'; 'Now put on your dress'.

REFLEX ACTIVITY LEVEL

- Prepare the clothing for (the person), ensure the dressing area is private and that a chair or bed at the right height is available for sitting.

- Talk through each stage of the activity as you put the clothing on to (the person). Use a calm tone, speak slowly and smile to indicate that you are nonthreatening.

- Stimulate a response in the limb being dressed by using firm but gentle stroking. Ask (the person) to assist you when necessary by using one-word requests: 'Lift'; 'Stand'; 'Sit'.

- At the end of dressing, spend some time brushing (the person's) hair using firm massaging brush strokes.

Activity: Bathing

PLANNED ACTIVITY LEVEL

- Encourage (the person) to plan when they will have the bath, to draw the water and select toiletries from the usual cupboard or shelf.

- Encourage (the person) to wash (his/her) own body; be available to assist if required.

- Encourage (the person) to release the water afterwards and to wipe the bath.

EXPLORATORY ACTIVITY LEVEL

- Break down the task into manageable chunks: suggest that (the person) fills the bath, then when that is accomplished suggest that he or she gathers together items such as soap, shampoo, flannel and towels.

- When (the person) is in the bath, suggest that (he/she) soaps and rinses (his/her) upper body and, when that is accomplished, suggest that (he/she) soaps and rinses (his/her) lower body.

- Ensure that bathing items are on view and that containers are clearly labelled.

- Have attractive objects around the bath such as unusual bath oil bottles or shells and encourage discussion and exploration of them.

SENSORY ACTIVITY LEVEL

- Prepare the bathroom and run the bath water for (the person).

- Make the bathroom warm and inviting – play music, use scented oils or bubble bath, have candles lit on a safely out-of-reach shelf.

- Break down the task into one step at a time and give (the person) simple directions: 'Rub the soap on the cloth, rub your arm, rinse your arm, rub your chest, rinse your chest…'

REFLEX ACTIVITY LEVEL

- Prepare the bathroom and run the bath water for (the person), put in scented bath products (lavender will aid relaxation).

- Ensure that the bathroom is warm and inviting. Make it feel secure by closing the door and curtains and providing a slip-resistant bath mat in the bath and on the floor. Clear away any unnecessary items which may be confusing.

- Use firm, massaging movements when soaping and rinsing (the person). Wrap (him/her) securely in a towel when (he/she) is out of the bath.

Activity: Dining

PLANNED ACTIVITY LEVEL

- Encourage (the person) to select when and what (he/she) wishes to eat.

- Encourage (the person) to prepare the dining-table and to select the cutlery, crockery and condiments from the usual cupboards or drawers.

- Encourage (the person) to clear away afterwards.

EXPLORATORY ACTIVITY LEVEL

- Store cutlery and crockery in view and encourage (the person) to select their own tools for dining.

- Offer food, using simple choices.

- Create a social atmosphere by using table decorations, music and so on, promoting conversation.

SENSORY ACTIVITY LEVEL

- Serve food so that it presents a variety of colours, tastes and textures.

- Offer (the person) finger foods; encourage (him/her) to feel the food.

- Offer (the person) a spoon, place it in (his/her) hand and direct (him/her) to 'Scoop the potato', 'Lift your arm', 'Open your mouth' and so on.

REFLEX ACTIVITY LEVEL

- Use touch on (the person's) forearm to make contact, maintain eye contact, and smile to indicate the pleasure of the activity.

- Place a spoon in (the person's) hand. Close your hand over (the person's) and raise the spoon with food on it to (his/her) mouth.

- As the food reaches (the person's) mouth say, 'Open' and open your own mouth to demonstrate. Touch (the person's) lips gently with the spoon.

THE POOL ACTIVITY LEVEL (PAL) OUTCOME SHEET

NAME:							
Activity:							
Date:	/ /	/ /	/ /	/ /	/ /	/ /	/ /
LEVEL OF ENGAGEMENT							
Goal aware							
Motivated							
Attention to detail							
Concentrates							
Appears interested							
Responds to sensations							
Explores objects							
PHYSICAL ABILITIES							
Standing/mobile							
Seated							
Uses tools							
Co-ordinated							
Grips objects							
Releases objects							
SOCIAL INTERACTION							
Aware of others							
Starts conversations							
Makes vocal noises							
Responds to others							
Aware of needs of others							
Shares in the group task							
Makes eye contact							
WELL-BEING							
Shows enjoyment							
Shows humour							
Assertive							
Makes choices							
Bored							
Angry							
Frightened							
Anxious							
Restless							
Sleepy							
KEY TO ACTIVITIES:	1. Personal ADL		2. Domestic ADL		3. Leisure		